Fruit in Fluted Bowl,
artist unknown, second
quarter of nineteenth
century, stencil and
watercolor, National
Gallery of Art, Gift
of Edgar William and
Bernice Chrysler Garbisch

The Art of America
from Jackson to Lincoln

By Shirley Glubok

DESIGNED BY GERARD NOOK

MACMILLAN PUBLISHING CO., INC.
New York
Collier Macmillan Publishers
London

The author gratefully acknowledges the kind assistance of:
Milton W. Brown, Professor of Art History, Graduate Division, City University of New York; *Jay E. Cantor*; *John K. Howat*, Curator, American Paintings and Sculpture, The Metropolitan Museum of Art; *Ellen Malino James*, Lecturer in American History, The New School for Social Research; *Weston J. Naef*, Assistant Curator, Department of Prints and Photographs, The Metropolitan Museum of Art; *Emma Papert*, Senior Librarian, The Metropolitan Museum of Art; *Louis Sharp*, Assistant Curator, American Paintings and Sculpture, The Metropolitan Museum of Art; *Natalie Spassky*, Assistant Curator, American Paintings and Sculpture, The Metropolitan Museum of Art; *Michael Pope*; and especially the helpful cooperation of *Stuart P. Feld* and *Marvin D. Schwartz*.

Other books by Shirley Glubok:

THE ART OF ANCIENT EGYPT	THE ART OF JAPAN
THE ART OF LANDS IN THE BIBLE	THE ART OF COLONIAL AMERICA
THE ART OF ANCIENT GREECE	THE ART OF THE SOUTHWEST INDIANS
THE ART OF THE NORTH AMERICAN INDIAN	THE ART OF THE OLD WEST
THE ART OF THE ESKIMO	THE ART OF THE NEW AMERICAN NATION
THE ART OF ANCIENT ROME	THE ART OF THE SPANISH IN THE
THE ART OF AFRICA	UNITED STATES AND PUERTO RICO
ART AND ARCHAEOLOGY	THE ART OF CHINA
THE ART OF ANCIENT PERU	THE FALL OF THE AZTECS
THE ART OF THE ETRUSCANS	THE FALL OF THE INCAS
THE ART OF ANCIENT MEXICO	DISCOVERING TUT-ANKH-AMEN'S TOMB
KNIGHTS IN ARMOR	DISCOVERING THE ROYAL TOMBS AT UR
THE ART OF INDIA	DIGGING IN ASSYRIA
HOME AND CHILD LIFE IN COLONIAL DAYS	

Front cover illustration: *Raftsmen Playing Cards,* by George Caleb Bingham, 1847, oil, The St. Louis Art Museum, Ezra H. Linley Fund. Back cover illustration: *Rainy Season in the Tropics,* by Frederick E. Church, 1866, oil, California Palace of the Legion of Honor.

Library of Congress Cataloging in Publication Data   Glubok, Shirley.   The art of America from Jackson to Lincoln.   1. Art—United States—History—Juvenile literature. [1. Art—United States—History]   I. Title.   N6510.G55   709'.73   72-81066   ISBN 0-02-736250-7

When Andrew Jackson was elected president in 1828, the thirteen original states had grown to twenty-four. "Old Hickory," as Jackson was called, was the first president to come to the White House from one of the new frontier states.

The Erie Canal recently had been completed, opening the way to the interior of the continent. New cities were rising along the great Western rivers, as older cities in the East expanded. Inventions and scientific discoveries prepared the way for new industries. The young United States, now free of European control, was growing powerful and prosperous.

A Smart Turnout, artist unknown, about 1845, oil, Wadsworth Atheneum, Hartford, Ella Gallup Sumner and Mary Catlin Sumner Collection

America's natural wonders inspired a group of artists to devote themselves to landscape painting. They wandered through hills and villages, through woods, meadows and farmlands, making sketches directly from nature. The group later became known as the "Hudson River school."

This scene is a view of the Oxbow, a bend in the Connecticut River, as seen from Mount Holyoke in Massachusetts, just after a storm. The twisted trees and crowded woods form a contrast to the tidy farmlands in the distance. The artist, Thomas Cole, has painted a tiny figure of himself in the foreground, working at his painter's easel.

1836, oil, The Metropolitan Museum of Art, Gift of Mrs. Russell Sage, 1908

5

Kindred Spirits, 1849, oil, The New York
Public Library, Astor, Lenox and Tilden Foundations

Cole and his friend, the poet William Cullen Bryant, were among the first to express their appreciation of America's wilderness through painting and poetry. The two often walked together in the Catskill Mountains in New York State.

In this painting by Asher Durand, they are shown standing together on a rock ledge overlooking a forest and a waterfall. Cole, the one in the hat, holds a sketch pad. Man's new interest in nature, which would become more and more important as the nineteenth century progressed, is symbolized in this painting.

At right, a shepherd and his flock seem lost in the forest. The trees and plants in the foreground are painted in careful detail.

The Beeches, by Asher B. Durand,
1845, oil, The Metropolitan Museum
of Art, Bequest of Maria de Witt Jesup, 1915

6

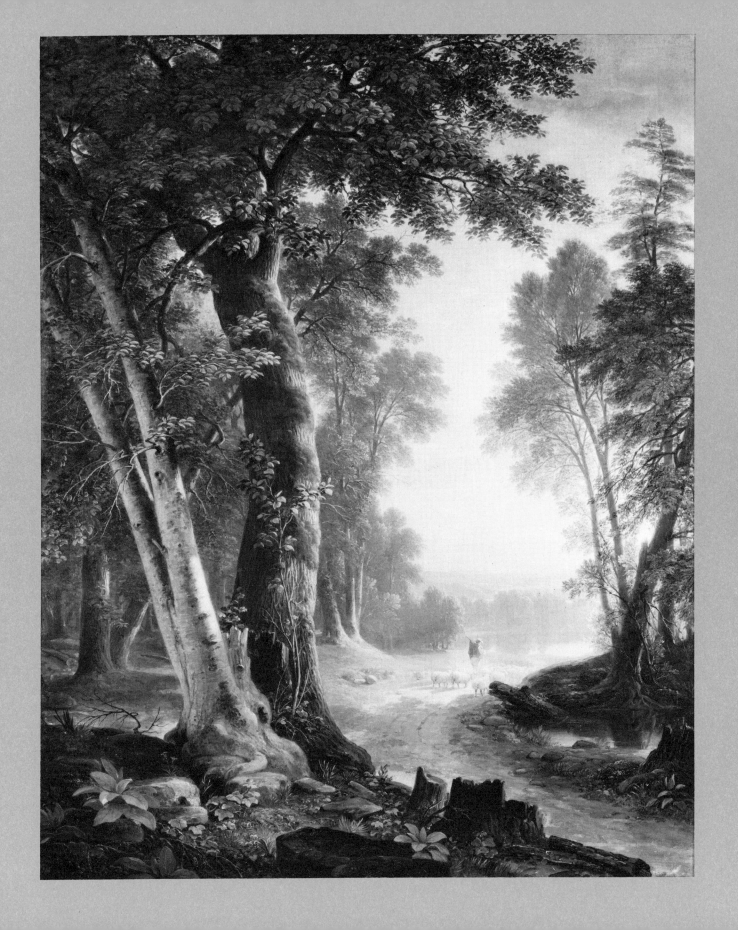

The Lackawanna Valley, 1855, oil, National Gallery of Art, Gift of Mrs. Huttleston Rogers

The year that Jackson was elected, the first horse-drawn railroad line began

operation, and in 1830 the first American steam locomotive made a successful run.

When a railroad company in Pennsylvania built its first roundhouse, George Inness

was asked to make a painting of it. The roundhouse, where each locomotive comes to the end of its run and turns around, can be seen in the background. But the painter was really more interested in the landscape: the fields, the factories, the village and the distant hills.

Boats were also an important means of transportation. In this view of Boston Harbor by Robert Salmon, the docks bustle with activity. Men in small boats pull at their oars, while large sailing vessels anchored in the harbor stand out against the sky. In the distance a view of the city skyline can be seen.

Boston Harbor from Constitution Wharf,
about 1842, oil, U.S. Naval Academy Museum

The invention of the steamboat, by the artist Robert Fulton, hastened the growth of cities on inland waterways. New Orleans, at the mouth of the Mississippi River, became an international trading center. Steamboats from ports along the rivers that flowed into the Mississippi ended their trips here. Sailing ships came through the Gulf of Mexico from all parts of the world to New Orleans. In the scene below by an unknown artist, the steamboat *Belle Creole* has just docked in the busy harbor.

Artist unknown, about 1850, oil, Corcoran Gallery of Art,
Gift of the Estate of Mrs. Emily Crane Chadbourne

Olivier Plantation, 1861, Louisiana State Museum

In the Southern states, great quantities of cotton and sugar cane were grown on large plantations. Life on a plantation in Louisiana is the subject of Adrian Persac's watercolor above. The mansion house and other plantation buildings are spread out on the spacious grounds. Groups of people stroll about as children set forth in a rowboat, on a beautiful day.

Maine in the summertime is the setting of this painting by Jerome B. Thompson.

Everyone from infant to grandmother is enjoying himself at a picnic. The artist

treated nature and people with equal importance in this pleasant scene.

Winter in New England was a favorite subject for the Connecticut painter

Sleighs Arriving at the Inn, 1851, oil, Private Collection

George Durrie. He liked to paint farmhouses and trees with bare branches covered

with snow. Durrie's landscape paintings include farmers with their animals,

carrying on their winter chores. Above, an ox drags a load of wood as sleighs

full of people arrive at an inn.

Many of Durrie's snow scenes were printed by Currier and Ives and became

familiar to people throughout the country.

Before photography was developed, artists often traveled from town to town painting portraits. *Mrs. Mayer and Daughter* is by the New England painter Ammi Phillips, who was self-taught. The artist has captured the character in the faces of his subjects. Phillips sometimes used the same composition over and over again by making the bodies the same but simply changing the faces.

Joseph Moore and his family gathered in the parlor for their portrait by Erastus Salisbury Field, a Massachusetts artist. He liked to paint patterned carpets,

About 1835, oil,
The Metropolitan Museum of Art,
Gift of Edgar William and
Bernice Chrysler Garbisch, 1962

About 1840, oil, Museum of Fine Arts, Boston,
M. and M. Karolik Collection

but the rest of the background is simple, so the figures stand out strongly. The

spools of thread on the small worktable and the needlework in Mrs. Moore's hands

show that she was an industrious woman.

Pat Lyon at the Forge, 1829, oil, Museum of Fine Arts, Boston, Deposited by the Boston Athenaeum

Patrick Lyon started his career as a blacksmith and then became a successful engineer and locksmith. When he had John Neagle paint his portrait, Lyon wanted to be shown in the smithy where he got his start. The building seen through the window is the Walnut Street jail in Philadelphia. It is a painful reminder of the time that Lyon had been sent there on a false charge.

Georgianna Buckham and her mother look soft, sweet and pretty, free from the cares of the world. The painter of this portrait, Henry Inman, often flattered his subjects and made them look better than they did in real life. Inman was a leading portrait artist in New York City, which was rapidly becoming the art center of America.

1839, oil, Museum of Fine Arts, Boston, Bequest of Georgianna Buckham Wright

1869, The Brooklyn Museum,
Gift of Mrs. Charles F. Bound

In the first half of the nineteenth century, many American sculptors went to live in Italy, where they could study ancient works of art and learn from Italian sculptors working in the ancient manner. There they could get beautiful marble from local quarries and have skilled Italian marble cutters work for them.

Hiram Powers was working in Florence when he made his famous marble statue, *The Greek Slave*. He used as his model an ancient Greek statue of Venus, the goddess of love. Powers's statue represents a young woman taken captive by the Turks, who had ruled Greece for almost four hundred years until the Greeks gained their independence in 1829. Americans, who only recently had fought and won their own revolutionary war, sympathized with the Greeks in their fight for freedom.

The life-size *Greek Slave* was exhibited in London in 1851 during the first World's Fair ever held. At right is a view of an art gallery in New York where the statue was also displayed. Powers made six life-size copies of the slave girl. Poems were written about the statue and small copies were made and displayed in homes all over the country. Powers was the first American sculptor to become internationally known.

Engraving by Robert Thew,
1858, The Metropolitan
Museum of Art, Gift of
Albert T. Gardner, 1971

19

Classical, or ancient Greek and Roman, architecture was copied by Americans, creating a style that became known as Greek Revival. Temples were used as models for state, federal and commercial buildings, banks and even penitentiaries throughout the United States.

The Merchants' Exchange in Philadelphia is in the Greek Revival style. The building was constructed on a triangular piece of ground and includes a post office, a reading room, business space and offices. The architect of the building, William Strickland, had his offices there. One hundred and forty

Built 1832–1835, lithograph by George Lehman
about 1836, The Historical Society of Pennsylvania

Andalusia, 1833, photograph by Wayne Andrews

men worked on the stone building, including twenty-seven Italian sculptors who carved the capitals, or tops of the columns. An ancient monument in Athens, Greece, was used as a model for the structure on the roof.

Even homes were built in the Greek Revival style. After the owner of this house on the Delaware River took a trip to Greece, he had the architect Thomas U. Walter make it look like a temple in Athens. Walter added to the house a portico, or porch, with wooden columns two stories tall. Over the columns he added the pediment, or triangular area, that hides the flat roof.

Greek influence can be seen everywhere in this parlor from Albany, New York. The marble top of a table against the wall stands on marble columns, the bases of which are shaped like lions' paws. The mantel over the fireplace is supported by carved female figures called caryatids. Even the chairs, with curved back rails and curved legs, are of ancient Greek design.

The style of furniture in this period is called Empire, named after the French style created for the Emperor Napoleon. The furniture in this room was made in New York. The rugs and many of the small objects were imported from France, including the clock on the mantel with the standing figure of George Washington.

The eagle, symbol of the new American nation, was widely used as a form of decoration. It can be seen on the clock, the frame of the oval mirror and the little shelf on the wall above the table.

An eagle also sits on top of this elegant cast-iron parlor stove that was made in Albany. The surface of the stove is decorated with acanthus leaves, a favorite Greek ornament.

By Low and Leake, patented 1844,
The Metropolitan Museum of Art,
Gift of Dick Button, 1969

About 1830, The Henry Francis
du Pont Winterthur Museum

Designed by Richard Upjohn, 1839–1846, lithograph by
John Forsyth and E. W. Mimee 1847, Museum of the City
of New York, The J. Clarence Davies Collection

Architects also turned to the Middle Ages for inspiration. Medieval cathedrals in the Gothic style served as models for buildings from cottages to universities. When Trinity Church in New York City was rebuilt, it was designed in the Gothic Revival style. Its slender spires, pointed arches, stained-glass windows and steeply pitched roofs are architectural forms borrowed from the Middle Ages.

Many styles of many periods often were combined in one building. Henry Austin designed a house in Portland, Maine, that is a blend of Rococo, Baroque and Renaissance styles of architecture.

An artist-decorator with eleven assistants designed the interior. All of the woodwork was hand-carved. A huge double chandelier hangs in the hallway. The house is known as the Victoria Mansion. Its elaborate decorations are typical of the Victorian age, the period from 1837 to 1901 when Queen Victoria ruled England.

1858

During the Victorian period, Americans adapted the fancy designs of King Louis XV of France into the Rococo Revival style. In this parlor from a house in New York state, the fireplace and mirror are heavily decorated. The chairs and sofa, with carved wooden frames and lush upholstery, were made to order for the owner of the house.

The room's crowded look is typical of Victorian parlors. Chairs are grouped around the table in the center of the room. Knickknacks fill the shelves and mantel and elegant draperies frame the tall windows. The floral pattern of the rug and the molding in the ceiling add to the cluttered feeling.

Even this silver kettle was made in the Rococo style. It was part of a silver tea service presented to the head of the company that ran the first telegraph lines from New York to Boston and Buffalo. On top of the kettle is a standing figure of Zeus, king of the gods in ancient Greece, encircled by telegraph poles and wires.

John Chandler Moore, about 1850,
The Metropolitan Museum of Art,
Gift of Mrs. F. R. Lefferts, 1969

From the Robert J. Milligan House,
Saratoga Springs, 1855,
The Brooklyn Museum

The simplicity of this room reflects the Shaker belief that the most useful is the most beautiful. The Shakers are members of a religious group which formed its own communities. Each object in their communal dwellings and meeting houses had to serve a purpose. Cupboards and drawers were built into the walls. Pegs were used for hanging bonnets and clothes. Oval wooden boxes, made of thin strips of maple, nested inside each other when not in use.

The Shakers were not permitted to decorate their dwellings. But when a Shaker had a dream or vision, it was recorded in an ink-and-watercolor "spirit drawing," as shown below.

1847, Index of American Design, National Gallery of Art

Dwelling room from Enfield, New Hampshire, about 1840,
The Henry Francis du Pont Winterthur Museum

29

The interior of an ordinary home is shown in the painting below. The artist, Francis William Edmonds, recorded every object in the room as carefully as he painted the people. A family interrupts its work to look at the wares of a peddler who has come to the house selling small plaster statues. Pictures that tell stories of everyday life are called genre paintings.

In *The Sailor's Wedding,* a proud young seaman has brought his bashful young lady to a magistrate to be married. The magistrate seems annoyed at having his lunch interrupted. Curious spectators watch through the open doorway. Every detail

About 1844, oil, The New-York Historical Society

of the room, including the wallpaper and the brass andirons, is painted carefully.

Richard Caton Woodville, the artist, grew up in Baltimore and then went to Düsseldorf, Germany, where he continued to paint American subjects.

Eel Spearing at Setauket, 1845, oil, New York State Historical Association, Cooperstown

William Sidney Mount, one of America's most important genre painters, never left America. He spent most of his life on Long Island, painting neighbors and friends at work and play. Above, a boy, with his dog beside him, paddles a boat while a woman stands in the prow with a long spear to catch eels. The boy's family, for whom the painting was made, live in the house in the background.

In this pleasant scene of workers resting in a field, Mount shows every detail of leaves, grass and haystack. Many of Mount's outdoor farm scenes were reproduced as prints and were widely circulated.

Farmers Nooning, 1836, oil, Suffolk Museum, Stony Brook, New York, Melville Collection

Outdoor scenes of Indian life were painted by Seth Eastman, an Army officer stationed in the West. Above, a group of Sioux are playing lacrosse, a game still played by the Indians today. The mountains form a background for the rough-and-tumble game.

George Catlin recorded the appearance and customs of Plains Indians before the coming of the Eastern settlers. Catlin journeyed up the Missouri River from St. Louis, visiting Indian settlements that had never been seen by a white man.

His paintings of Indians have dignity and beauty. Below is Om-pah-ton-ga, the Big Elk, chief of the Omaha tribe. Catlin exhibited his Indian portraits in Eastern cities and in Europe. At some of the exhibits, Indians performed tribal dances.

1833, oil, National
Collection of Fine Arts,
Smithsonian Institution

A young Indian hunter and his dog are the subjects of this realistic bronze statue by John Quincy Adams Ward. Unlike most other sculptors of his time, Ward stayed in America all his life. He was working in New York when he decided to travel west to the Dakotas to study the Indians. While in the West, he made sketches and wax models which he took back to New York to make

About 1860, formerly in the Collection of Mrs. R. Ostrander Smith, photograph by Bob Zucker

this statue, which is only sixteen inches high. Ward used it as a model for life-size bronze statues that stand in parks in New York City and Buffalo and Cooperstown, New York, and over Ward's grave in Urbana, Ohio.

Lafayette Park in Washington, D.C., across from the White House, is the setting for this large bronze statue of General Andrew Jackson astride a rearing horse. The statue is remarkable because the whole weight of the horse and rider rests on the horse's slender hind legs.

Clark Mills, the sculptor, built his own foundry to cast this statue. At a foundry, bronze is heated until it becomes liquid. The metal is then poured into a mold prepared by the sculptor. Mills's foundry was one of the first in America.

The statue celebrates General Jackson's victory over the British at the Battle of New Orleans in the War of 1812. An old cannon that he had captured in the battle was melted down to supply the bronze for the sculpture. Mills kept a horse in a stable in his backyard in Washington, D.C., to use as a model.

1848–1853,
photograph by Alfred Tamarin

About 1837, crayon, Collection of Mr. and Mrs. J. Maxwell Moran

The painting at right by William Tylee Ranney captures the action of a cowboy lassoing wild horses. The animals' bulging eyes and their flying manes and tails add to the excitement of the scene.

The crayon drawing above is a sketch that was used as a study for one of the horses in this painting.

Ranney had been an illustrator and portrait painter in New York, then volunteered for the army in Texas and fought in the war that brought Texas independence from Mexico. While stationed there, he sketched hunters, trappers, scouts and animals. When he returned to the East, he used these Western sketches as studies for oil paintings of the rough life of the Texas frontier.

Hunting Wild Horses, 1846, oil, Northern Natural
Gas Company Collection, Joslyn Art Museum, Omaha

In 1848 news from the Pacific Coast reached the East: gold had been discovered in California. Farmers and city people by the thousands left their work and started west to look for gold. Flocks of European immigrants joined the rush. In two years ninety thousand people traveled to California.

In *The Forty-niners,* two prospectors with camping and mining equipment look out over the mountains where they hope to find their fortune.

An earlier group of pioneers is the subject of a painting by George Caleb Bingham, a Missouri artist. Shortly before the Revolutionary War, Daniel

Boone had blazed the Wilderness Trail through the Appalachians into the land south of the Ohio River. In the painting, the famous frontiersman leads the settlers into Kentucky.

Daniel Boone Escorting Settlers Through the Cumberland Gap,
1851–1852, Washington University Gallery of Art

During the nineteenth century, there was an increasing interest in science. In this family portrait by Robert Weir, the father squints through a microscope, holding his less powerful magnifying glass aside. His wife and children watch with fascination.

The Microscope, 1849, oil, Yale University Art Gallery, John Hill Morgan and Olive Louise Dann Funds

The first practical method of photography was developed by Louis Daguerre, a French painter and theatrical scene designer. "Photography" comes from Greek words that mean "writing with light." In Daguerre's process, an image was recorded on a silvered copper plate by exposure to light, then fixed, or made permanent, by chemical action. The result was called a daguerreotype.

1848, The Metropolitan Museum of Art, Gift of I. N. Phelps Stokes, Edward S. Hawes, Alice Mary Hawes, Marion Augusta Hawes, 1937

Samuel F. B. Morse, the American painter and inventor of the telegraph, was in Paris at the time that Daguerre's process was announced. He brought the technique back to the United States. Soon photographers all over the country were making daguerreotypes.

This portrait of John Quincy Adams was made by Southworth and Hawes, the most important daguerreotype photographers of their day. It was taken when Adams was an old man, twenty years after he had completed his term as president of the United States and had been succeeded by Andrew Jackson.

The daguerreotype process produced only a single positive picture, which could not be used to make additional prints. It was soon replaced by a new photographic process that produced a negative from which any number of positive prints could be made.

Mathew Brady set up photographic studios in New York and Washington, and every important person of the day came to be photographed. When President Abraham Lincoln posed with his son Tad, the photographer gave the child a picture album to look at, to keep him still while the slow photographic plate was being exposed.

During the Civil War, Lincoln gave Brady and his staff permission to go into the battlefields. Brady and his assistants took several thousand photographs of the men, the camps and the battlegrounds, making a complete pictorial record of the war. This photograph of soldiers who were wounded in the battle of Fredericksburg points up the tragedies of war.

In the early days of photography, photographs could not be printed in magazines because the process of photoengraving was not yet widely used. Magazines used pictures that were printed from wood blocks into which the image was engraved by hand. Ink was spread on the wood, then paper was pressed over it, printing the picture.

During the Civil War, *Harper's Weekly* assigned a young artist-reporter, Winslow Homer, to cover the Union armies. This wood engraving of a soldier taking aim from a tree was based upon a drawing Homer had made in the battlefield.

It was probably a magazine illustration that inspired John Rogers to do this statue group of two wounded soldiers who have been ordered to the rear during a battle. One of them is determined to have one more shot before retreating. Due to its subject matter this bronze statuette was a favorite gift for veterans of the Civil War.

Rogers had a factory where he produced hundreds of copies of his statuettes. They were usually made of plaster so they could be sold cheaply.

Wounded to the Rear—One More Shot,
1865, The Metropolitan Museum of Art,
Rogers Fund, 1917

The years between Jackson's election and Lincoln's death were years of rapid growth and development for the United States, and the art of the period vividly reflects the excitement of the times.

By 1865, when the Civil War ended, the American nation stretched across the entire continent, from the Atlantic Ocean to California on the Pacific. The United States, which already had begun to open doorways in the world for its expanding commerce, was on its way to becoming a major world power.

Pierre, by Alfred Jacob Miller, about 1860, watercolor, The Walters Art Gallery

J
N6510
.G55

Glubok
The art of America from
Jackson to Lincoln.

The Date Due Card in the pocket indicates the date on or before which this book should be returned to the Library.

Please do not remove cards from this pocket.